HOUGHTON MIFFLIN HARCOURT
School Publishers

From *Judy Moody* by Megan McDonald, illustrated by Peter H. Reynolds. Text Copyright © 2000 by Megan McDonald, illustrations copyright © 2000 by Peter H. Reynolds. Reprinted by permission of Candlewick Press, Santillana Publishing Company, Inc. and the author. "Fast Track" by Nikki Grimes. Copyright © 1999 by Nikki Grimes. Reprinted by permission of Curtis Brown Ltd. "Ode to My Shoes" from *From the Bellybutton of the Moon and Other Summer Poems/ Del ombligo de la luna y otras poemas de verano*. Copyright © 1998 by Francisco X. Alarcón. Reprinted by permission of the publisher, Children's Book Press, San Francisco, CA, www.childrensbookpress.org. "Magnet" from *All The Small Poems and Fourteen More* by Valerie Worth. Text copyright © 1994 by Valerie Worth. Reprinted by permission of Farrar, Straus and Giroux LLC. "Science Fair Project" from *Almost Late to School and More School Poems* by Carol Diggory Shields. Text copyright © 2003 by Carol Diggory Shields. All rights reserved including the right of reproduction in whole or in part in any form. Reprinted by permission of Dutton Books, a member of Penguin Young Readers Group, a division of Penguin Group (USA) Inc., and Carol Diggory Shields. "I chop chop chop without a stop..." from *Good Sports* by Jack Prelutsky. Text copyright © 2007 by Jack Prelutsky. Reprinted by permission of Alfred A. Knopf, an imprint of Random House Children's Books, a division of Random House, Inc. "Long Jump" from *Swimming Upstream: Middle School Poems* by Kristine O'Connell George. Text copyright © 2002 by Kristine O'Connell George. Reprinted by permission of Houghton Mifflin Harcourt Publishing Company and the author. "Defender" from *Tap Dancing on the Roof: Sijo (Poems)* by Linda Sue Park. Text copyright © 2007 by Linda Sue Park. Reprinted by permission of Houghton Mifflin Harcourt Publishing Company and Curtis Brown Ltd. "Spellbound" from *The Dog Ate My Homework* by Sara Holbrook. Text copyright © 1996 by Sara Holbrook. Reprinted by permission of Boyds Mills Press, Inc. "Company's Coming" from *The Alligator in the Closet and Other Poems Around the House* by David L. Harrison. Text copyright © 2003 by David L. Harrison. Reprinted by permission of Wordsong, a division of Boyds Mills Press Inc.

Printed in the U.S.A.

ISBN: 978-0-547-86440-2

3 4 5 6 7 8 9 10 0930   20 19 18 17 16 15 14 13 12

4500365869   A B C D E F G

READING Adventures

Theme 1

The ROBODOGS of Greenville

by Thomas S. Park   illustrated by John Hovell

Characters

Narrator	Cosmo	Professor
Diz	Robodog	Captain Spacely

SCENE 1
Setting: Diz's house

Narrator: This story takes place in the year 2222 in a small town called Greenville. Greenville is a friendly little community, just like many other towns. Everyone gets along there.

Diz: Hi, Cosmo! Thanks for coming over.

Cosmo: Anytime, Diz! How are things over at your dad's hydro car store?

Diz: Really busy, Cosmo.

Cosmo: I hear they're selling those hydro cars faster than the factory on planet Mars can make them!

Narrator: Diz and Cosmo live with their families in Greenville. Their parents fly the children to school in the family hydro cars. The children chat with their friends each evening on the family televideocomputers. They also play with their family dogs.

Diz: Here, Robodog! Catch the flying disk!

Robodog: I am coming, Owner Diz. I will catch the disk.

Narrator: There is one unusual thing about the dogs in Greenville. All the dogs are robots.

Diz: Good catch, Robodog.

Robodog: Thank you, Owner Diz. What can I do for you now?

Narrator: The robodog is the only kind of dog in Greenville. Scientists have built robodogs to be better than real dogs. They can speak. They can take care of chores such as cleaning and cooking. They can even beam movies from their eyes onto a wall.

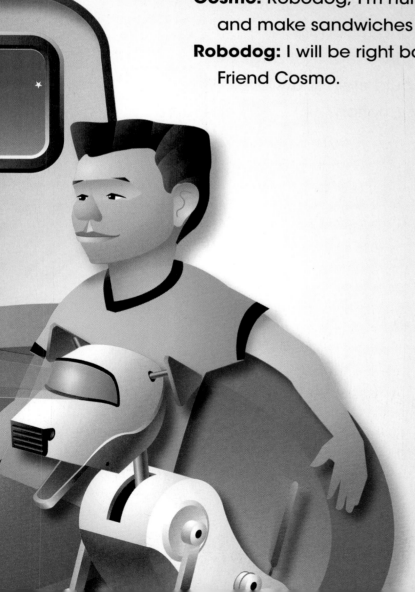

Cosmo: Last night, our robodog showed us an old movie.

Diz: What was it about?

Cosmo: It was about a real dog. She was beautiful!

Diz: A real dog? What was she like?

Cosmo: A lot like our robodogs. She could do tricks and help her owners.

Diz: Could she speak?

Cosmo: She could only make a sound called barking. She didn't know any human words.

Diz: Really? That's strange.

Robodog: Yes. That is very strange, Owner Diz.

Cosmo: Robodog, I'm hungry. Would you go to the kitchen and make sandwiches for Diz and me, please?

Robodog: I will be right back, Owner Diz and Friend Cosmo.

Cosmo: The dog in the movie seemed to love her owner. She was sweet and cuddly. She didn't just work around the house.

Diz: The dog loved her owner? I wish my robodog were like that.

Narrator: You see, robodogs are helpful and can do tricks, but they are not sweet or cuddly.

Cosmo: Maybe we should talk to the professor about this.

> **SCENE 2**
> **Setting:** The professor's house

Narrator: The professor is an expert on animals. So Diz and Cosmo go to talk to the professor about the differences between real dogs and robodogs.

Professor: Yes, Diz and Cosmo. It's true that real dogs could be happy or sad. They could even show love.

Diz: Why don't our robodogs show emotion?

Dog — Happy — Sad

Robodog — No Emoti

Professor: Scientists don't know how to make dogs that act like friends. They can make them useful, but not loving.

Cosmo: My robodog cleans my room, makes my meals, and helps me with my homework.

Diz: Robodogs aren't very cuddly!

Cosmo: I know. After Robodog has done its chores or tricks, it just switches off.

Professor: That's right. It dozes. The scientists made robodogs that way to save energy.

Diz: I wish I had a real dog.

Cosmo: There aren't any more real dogs. They disappeared permanently from Earth a hundred years ago.

Professor: It's funny that you should say that. I just got off my Intergalactic Computer Phone with the famous explorer Captain Spacely. He told me about an astonishing discovery. Maybe he can tell you about it, too. Computer Phone, call Captain Spacely.

Spacely: Captain Spacely here. Professor, do you want to hear more about my discovery?

Professor: Yes, indeed I do, Captain. Tell my friends Diz and Cosmo what you have found.

Spacely: I can do better than that. I'll show them what I've found!

Narrator: Captain Spacely steps away from the computer phone. Diz and Cosmo hear a whining sound. Then they hear barking.

Diz: What is that strange sound?

Cosmo: I heard that sound in the movie. It's the barking sound a real dog makes!

Narrator: Captain Spacely is visible on the screen again. He beckons to a furry thing that leaps into his arms. Cosmo and Diz see that it looks something like a robodog, but it acts differently.

Spacely: I've found real dogs! There is a small planet that has many of the same animals that were once on Earth. In fact, it has so many kinds of animals that food and space are becoming hard to find.

Narrator: The dog in Captain Spacely's arms wags its tail and licks his face. Diz and Cosmo look at the dog with amazement.

Diz: I wish I could have one of those dogs!

Cosmo: Me, too!

Professor: I think that can be arranged. Tell them your plan, Captain Spacely!

Spacely: To help the animals, I am bringing a spaceship full of dogs back to Earth! There is lots of room on Earth for dogs. Cosmo and Diz, if you promise to care for them, you can have the first two!

Diz and Cosmo: Thanks, Captain Spacely!

SCENE 3
Setting: Diz's house

Narrator: Sure enough, Captain Spacely brings real dogs back to Earth. Cosmo and Diz get the first two dogs.

Diz: Give me a hug, Scooter!

Cosmo: Here, Rascal! Come and play with me!

Narrator: As for the robodogs, Cosmo and Diz decide to keep them. They come in handy when it is time to give Scooter and Rascal a bath.

Robodog: Owner Cosmo, should I get Rascal's bath ready?

Cosmo: Yes, Robodog. After that, would you take Rascal out for a walk?

Tell Me When Tell Me Where

When you tell about something that happened, it is important to use words that tell **when** events happened. Time-order words such as *before*, *after,* and *then* help your listener understand the order of events.

> *After Robodog has done its chores or tricks, it just switches off.*

What word in this sentence helps you understand when Robodog switches off?

To give your listeners a clear picture, you also need to include words that tell **where** things are or where they happened.

> *Would you go to the kitchen and make sandwiches for Diz and me, please?*

What words in the sentence tell you where Robodog goes?

With a partner, take turns telling about an event in *The Robodogs of Greenville,* using words that tell *when* and *where*.

Have Your Say

Think about an experience you have had with an animal. It could be a pet or even an unusual zoo animal. Describe to your classmates what the animal was like and how you felt. Were you excited or afraid?

Before you talk about your experience, you will need to:
- think about details and words that describe how you felt.

As you are speaking, remember to:
- speak clearly in complete sentences.

As you are listening to one another speak, remember to:
- listen carefully so that you can ask questions when the speaker has finished.

When you are finished speaking, your classmates will ask you questions.

Good writers use time-order words and phrases such as *before, after, then,* and *last week* to help their readers understand the order of events in their writing.

In *The Robodogs of Greenville,* Cosmo and Diz are surprised that Captain Spacely discovered real dogs on another planet. Later, they are even more surprised when they receive the first two real dogs. The letter below is about another surprise. How do the time-order words and phrases in the letter help you understand the order of events?

Dear Justin,

You won't believe what happened to me last week! My mom left me clues for a treasure hunt. First, I had to go to the living room. Next, I had to go to the kitchen. Finally, I had to go to the basement. After a few seconds, I heard a funny sound. I walked toward the sound, where I found a new kitten waiting for me. I named the kitten Mia. I hope you will be able to meet her soon.

Sincerely,
Kayla

Reflect on Your Writing

Choose a friendly letter or a personal narrative that you have completed in class. As you read your writing, ask yourself these questions.

✓ Is it easy to understand the order of events in my writing?

✓ Where should I add words that tell about time order such as *before, after, then,* or *last week*?

✓ Where can I combine choppy sentences and make them compound sentences?

Answer the questions, and then edit your writing.

LIGHTS, CAMERA, ACTION!

The History of Movies

by Chris Bennett

Lights, camera, action! When you hear those words you think of movies. Just over one hundred years ago, movies were very different than they are today.

The first motion pictures in the late 1800s were moving pictures with no sound. They were only about a minute long. The early inventors worked hard to make moving pictures better. They designed new cameras to take pictures and record them on film, and projectors to show the pictures. Their designs and ideas led to today's movies, which are the most exciting and amazing movies ever!

Edison's Kinetoscope

Thomas Edison

The very first step toward making movies was the invention of photography in the 1820s. Photography is the process of making pictures with a camera. After this, inventors in the United States and other countries wanted a way to show motion, or the act of moving. The race was on!

One of the first people to succeed was an American, Thomas Edison. In 1889, he and his assistant, William Dickson, invented the kinetoscope. The kinetoscope used a camera, film, and an electric lamp.

Inside a four-foot high wooden box, a loop of film ran through a special camera. An electric lamp under the film lit images on the film as it passed through the camera. Our eyes see the quick movement of the images as motion. A peephole at the top of the box allowed a single person to view the moving pictures. At a kinetoscope parlor, the public watched motion pictures for the very first time.

In the 1890s, kinetoscope parlors opened all across the United States. At a parlor, a customer could view a different film in five different kinetoscopes for five cents each.

Auguste and Louis Lumière

The Lumières' Motion-Picture Projector

In Paris, Charles Antoine Lumière saw a movie through Edison's kinetoscope. He was impressed, but he believed his sons could design a better way to watch movies. His sons, Auguste and Louis, were two of the smartest scientists in Paris. They noticed one big problem with Edison's kinetoscope. Only one person could view the film at a time.

The Lumière brothers invented a camera and a projector that was one machine. They called their invention a *cinematographe*. The *cinematographe* recorded images on film which could be projected onto a screen. Many people could now sit together and watch larger moving images. The Lumières showed their movies to the public much like movie theaters do today.

This new entertainment was different and exciting. Nothing like it had ever been seen before!

The Lumière brothers presented their first motion picture show in December, 1895. Soon, they were showing their motion pictures in cities all over the world.

Nickelodeon storefront theater from the early 1900s

Early Movies and Movie Theaters

Soon, smaller, lighter movie projectors were being made in the United States. Movies became part of fairgrounds and "traveling tent" shows all over the country. The moving pictures had no sound, so narrators and musicians often traveled with the shows. They told the story and added music and sound effects to the moving pictures.

In 1902, *A Trip to the Moon* was one of the first movies that told a story.

The first movie theaters in the U.S were called *nickelodeons*. These small theaters charged a nickel to watch a movie. Movies, called *shorts*, were only about 15 minutes long. In a nickelodeon, a piano player often played along to the film as the audience watched.

What Next? Sound!

Even though there was no sound in early films, movies became more and more popular. In silent films, an actor's words were printed on the film and projected onto the screen, like words on a page.

The next challenge was to have sound to go with the images on the screen. People wanted to hear movies as well as see them. Moviemakers had always been interested in sound. The invention of a new kind of film in 1919 made sound on film possible. A camera was able to record images and sound on film at the same time. At first, the quality of the sound was poor. After many experiments, the quality improved. Big movie theaters started buying expensive sound systems. The public was very excited to hear what the actors were saying.

The new movies with sound were called *talkies*. The first full-length talkie was *The Jazz Singer* in 1927. The movie had both music and speaking. It was a smash success! Movies would never be silent again.

The Jazz Singer was the first feature film with dialogue and music.

The Wizard of Oz had lots of color!

Color Films

Another big step in the history of movies was adding color to film. Just as with sound, making movies with a lot of color took some time to get right. In some very early movies, color was painted onto film, frame by frame. Imagine a hand-painted film! Another method was to tint film by dipping it into a dye.

By the 1930s, a better process was used to make color movies. It used three layers of special color film. Each layer of film was a separate color. Together, they made all the colors.

One of the first color movies using the new process was *The Wizard of Oz* in 1939. This movie still looks great! Later, less expensive color film and cameras were designed.

Special Effects

For most of their history, movies have had special effects. These are tricks that make things seem different than they really are. Moviemakers can do amazing things with special effects.

Blue screen photography is a common special effect. Using blue screens, an actor can seem to be at the top of the Empire State Building, or flying over the Grand Canyon. The trick is that the actor never leaves the movie studio!

How does it happen? First, the actor is filmed in front of a blue screen. Next, a film of a background, such as the Grand Canyon, is made. Then the two pieces of film are put together to look like one very real scene.

Another special effect is called *slow motion*. A slow motion camera films action at a faster camera speed than normal. When a projector plays the film at normal speed, the action appears to slow down.

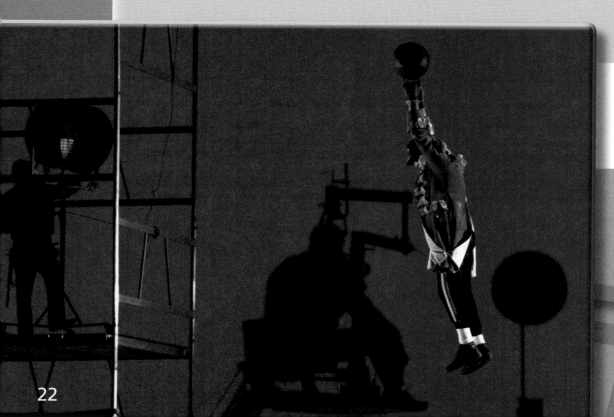

This actor is posing in front of a blue screen.

Today, most movie special effects are done using high-tech video cameras and computers. The process is called *CGI,* which means "computer-generated imagery." In 1993 *Jurassic Park* brought dinosaurs to life in a way that wowed audiences. Later, *Avatar* showed life on an imaginary planet in new ways. These movies could never have been made at an earlier time. In fact, the whole movie experience has changed a lot in just the last twenty years.

Now you can watch a 3-D movie in a special large theater with surround sound. Your seat moves back to view the action on a dome screen 72 feet high! In some theaters, you can even have dinner served with your movie.

Movies have come a long way since the silent movie shorts of the nickelodeon. Today's movies are much more thrilling than the first silent movies.

The movie *King Kong* was made in 1933. It had great special effects for a movie of its time, and it was a big hit with adult audiences. Sixty years later, *Jurassic Park* thrilled moviegoers with life-like dinosaurs.

Media Maze

When your parents went to school and wanted to find information on a topic, they may have read books, newspapers, and magazines. Today there are many other ways to find information.

Suppose you wanted to research movie special effects. You could still use books, magazines, or newspapers. You could also use many different kinds of media for your research. You could:

- search the Internet for websites about special effects.

- watch a video clip of a makeup artist working with an actor.

- study charts and graphs that give information about numbers or dates related to special effects.

- watch a TV show about the history of special effects.

As you explore different types of media, look for the main ideas and details in the information you find. This will help you understand and organize the information.

Media Presentations

1 Work with a partner or a small group. Choose and research a topic related to movies, such as silent movies, special effects, or cartoons.

2 Choose a type of media mentioned on the previous page to find information on your topic.

3 Note the main ideas and details in the material you select.

4 Present your findings to the class. Be sure to explain clearly the main ideas and details in your presentation.

5 Include a picture, a chart, a graph, or a short video clip to help support your presentation.

File   Edit   View   Favorites   Tools   Help

Search

Special Effects in the Movies

What's New | Trade Shows | Artist Spotlight | Awards

The latest monster movie is coming out with all the latest effects.

 **Your Turn**

The Right Words Matter

CONNECTING WORDS

Good writers make their ideas clear to their readers. They use connecting words and phrases, such as *because*, *since*, and *for example,* to link their opinion and reasons.

What is the writer's opinion in the sentence below? What is the connecting word?

Special effects are astonishing because they make your imagination come alive.

WORDS AND PHRASES FOR EFFECT

Good writers also choose words and phrases that will cause their audience to feel a certain way.

What word does the author use for effect in the sentence below?

3-D movies are incredible.

Reflect on Your Writing

Choose the response to literature you wrote in this unit or another response piece. Look over your writing. Ask yourself these questions:

- Did I use connecting words to link my opinion and the reasons for my opinion?

- Where can I state my opinions and reasons more clearly?

- Where can I add words or phrases for effect?

Answer the questions and then edit your

Technology Wins the Game

by Mark Andrews

Almost everyone loves a good game. However, it's not just athletic ability or skill that helps sports players win. Many other things can contribute to a winning team or player. One of those things is the use of technology. Technology has made our lives easier and better in many ways. In sports, technology can help all types of athletes perform better.

It's All in the Design

If you like sports and science, being a sports engineer might be the job for you. Sports engineers are scientists who make sports more fun to play and to watch. They design better materials, surfaces, and equipment. They help keep athletes safe from injury. A sports engineer has probably helped to improve your favorite sport!

The Science of Sports Engineering

Some sports engineers study the way athletes move when they play different sports. An engineer might watch a soccer player to see how the player's foot strikes the ball. This can lead to ideas about soccer shoes, the soccer ball, or even the soccer field. Engineers use these ideas to improve the game in some way.

The first step for a sports engineer is to identify a problem in a sport—something to be improved. Almost anything can be improved! Then the sports engineer comes up with a possible solution. Next, he or she creates a model. The model may include a new kind of material. The new idea is then tested in a laboratory to see how well it works. Finally, the new product is tested by athletes. If it works well, soon athletes around the world will start to use it.

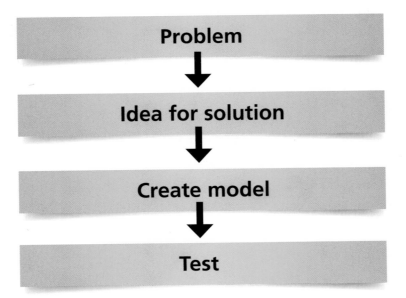

Problem

⬇

Idea for solution

⬇

Create model

⬇

Test

Changing the Game

Let's take a look at tennis. This is a sport where sports engineers have made several changes.

What a Racket!

Tennis rackets have changed a lot. When the sport began, tennis rackets were made out of wood. Then in the 1960s, a metal racket was developed. Metal rackets were stronger and lighter than wood. Today, rackets are made out of different materials mixed together. These rackets are very light and provide more power than the old ones. The ball moves faster than ever.

Today's rackets also have a larger head, or string area, than before. This makes it easier for the tennis player to reach more balls. A player can also control the ball better and make it move in different ways.

More Bounce to the Ball

Tennis balls have come a long way, too. The first tennis balls were made of leather or cloth stuffed with wool or horsehair. These balls did not bounce very high. In the 1870s, rubber was first used to make tennis balls. These balls bounced better, but the cloth that covered the ball would fall off.

Today, tennis balls are still made of rubber. First, two matching "half-shell" pieces of rubber are joined together. This makes the hollow, round shape of the ball. Second, two pieces of felt are wrapped around the ball. Third, a rubber seam is added to keep the felt cover together. Finally, the balls are put in a can that is under pressure. This helps keep them bouncy. The whole process ensures that each tennis ball bounces the exact same way. Where the ball bounces is up to the player!

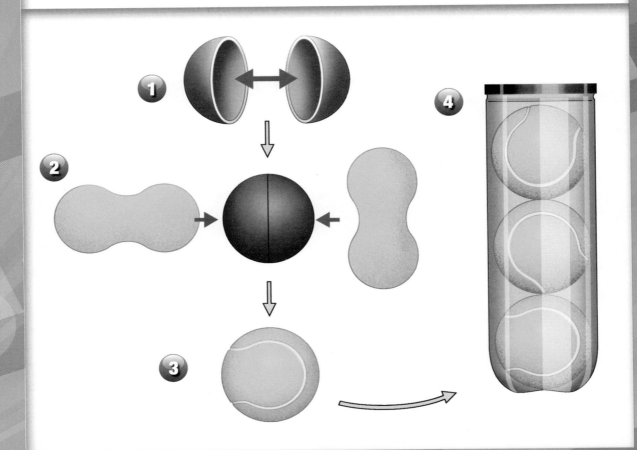

Higher and Faster

Sports engineers help athletes perform in just about every sport. Track and field athletes run, jump, and throw. Sports engineers help these athletes run faster, jump higher, and throw farther. They design new and better track and field equipment, surfaces, and clothing.

Jump Higher

Have you ever watched a pole vaulter at the Olympics? A good pole vaulter must have speed, strength, and the right pole. The pole must be flexible and strong enough to bend and lift the vaulter over the bar. Poles used to be made of wood. These were very stiff and heavy. Later, poles were made of more flexible bamboo. Then engineers designed poles made of aluminum. Today, poles are made of fiberglass and are very light. They bend easily. The more the pole bends, the further the vaulter sails through the air.

Run Faster

What makes a runner fast? Athletic ability and good training are most important. Engineers have designed new track surfaces and clothing to help.

Track runners used to run on grass fields. When it rained, the tracks would become soggy and slippery. Now, most runners run on "all-weather" tracks. These are man-made surfaces with a top coating of rubber chips. The rubber chips make the runners' shoes bounce off the track better. This increases speed.

New kinds of clothing also help runners speed up. Track stars don't wear shirts and shorts like they used to. They wear light-weight body suits that fit tightly. When they run in these suits, the wind does not slow them down. Every fraction of a second counts!

A New Kind of Racing

The Boston Marathon is the oldest and most famous marathon race in the world. Each year thousands of athletes run the 26-mile course through the hilly streets of Boston.

In 1975, Bob Hall finished the marathon in a different way. He wheeled his way to the finish line. Bob Hall was the first official wheelchair athlete to complete the Boston Marathon. He finished the race in less than 3 hours, faster than most runners.

▲ Bob Hall used a simple wheelchair in the Boston Marathon.

Today, wheelchair athletes compete with high-tech wheelchairs. ▶

In *These* Shoes?

Sport engineers have also designed athletes' shoes to make them faster and quicker and to give them more support. Athletes need different kinds of shoes for different sports. If you want to win, you need the right shoes!

A History of Running Shoes

In ancient times, runners ran barefoot. As time went on, athletes began to run in sandals. Soon, the sandal wearers were winning most of the races. The running shoe was born.

The next big change came in the 1800s in England. The first running shoe with a rubber sole was introduced. Rubber soles were light and comfortable. They also gripped the ground easily.

In the 1920s, a German named Adi Dassler sold the first modern running shoes with spikes. Spikes grip the ground and increase running speed.

Today, shoemakers and engineers better understand the science of running. Running shoes are made for every style of runner and any surface. Engineers know that runners need shoes that are strong and flexible.

Changes in Running Shoes

5th century B.C.
Ancient Greece: bare feet and sandals

1800s
shoes with rubber soles for a better grip

1920s
modern spiked running shoes

1979
air bubbles in sole for cushioning

2010
foam, silicone, air, gel cushioned shoes

Extra Bounce

Long jumpers need shoes that give the athletes extra bounce. The soles must be firm, but able to bend. These shoes have metal spikes in the front of the shoe only. This helps the jumper grip the ground and spring from the toes right before the jump.

Quick Movement

Soccer shoes have plastic or metal cleats, or rounded spikes, on the bottom. Cleats keep soccer players from slipping in the dirt, grass, and mud. Soccer players need to change directions quickly. Without cleats, soccer would be a slower, sloppier game!

Play Safely

Athletes also need special equipment and clothing to protect them from injury. Sports can be dangerous, and professional athletes often take risks.

Football Helmets

Over 100 years ago, football players did not wear helmets. Ouch! Then in the 1900s, players began to wear leather helmets. These early helmets did not provide much comfort or protection. Changes were needed. First, more padding was added. Second, a face mask was added to protect the nose and teeth. Also, the top of the helmet was made more round. This allowed a blow to slide off the helmet rather than strike head-on. Next, in 1939, the first plastic helmet was invented.

Today's football helmets are made of a special plastic that is light and strong. The helmet design protects players from head injuries. Some football helmets have tiny computer chips inside them. If a player hits his head, the chip sends a message to a computer on the sideline. The message helps doctors and coaches know if the player needs help.

Other Safety Features

Some ski clothes are made to help skiers in trouble. Sometimes back country skiers get lost or are injured miles away from anyone. Sports engineers developed special sensors for their clothing. The sensors send information about a skier's location. A rescue team receives the information. Then, they can find skiers who have fallen or are buried under the snow.

Brightly colored jackets and vests, called reflective wear, make bicyclists easier to see in the dark.

⬤ Just for Fun

The next time you play your favorite sport, think about some of the equipment you use. Think about the kind of surface you are standing, running, or jumping on. Notice how your sports shoes look or feel or help you perform. Now that you have read about sports engineering, you will probably think about how technology has helped to improve your sport. Technology not only makes our lives easier and better, but it also makes our lives a lot more fun!

Activity Central

Pleased, Happy, or Thrilled?

Some words, such as *pleased,* *happy,* and *thrilled,* have similar meanings. If you think about it, they are not exactly the same. When have you been pleased? happy? thrilled? Good writers and speakers choose words carefully so their audience will understand exactly what they mean. Read the words under the line. Which word sounds the least certain? the most certain?

thought　　　**wondered**　　　**believed**　　　**knew**

Read the sentences below. What is the meaning of each underlined word?

I <u>wondered</u> why you wanted to buy those shoes.

I just <u>knew</u> these new running shoes were going to help me run fast.

I <u>thought</u> your old shoes might be a problem.

thrilled
happy
pleased
content
sorry
gloomy
sad
unhappy

Rewrite the sentences below, filling in the blanks with words from the word bank. Then share your sentences with a partner. Ask your partner what word he or she chose for each sentence.

I am _____ track and field day is almost over.

Do you feel _____ about the 50-yard dash?

I am _____ with how I did.

Bring it to Life!

Good writers use clear, descriptive language to tell about the thoughts, feelings, and actions of people in a story. They use descriptive words and details to make the events and experiences come alive for their audience! As you read the paragraph below, notice the descriptive details. How does the writer describe the ball going over the goal? How does the writer feel about the game?

I waited eagerly all week for the soccer game to begin. The teams raced down the field. My teammates and I quickly chased the ball. I cornered the ball as I sprinted down the field. I swerved suddenly to my right and shifted my foot behind the ball. I kicked it straight at the net. The ball sailed high over the goal. I swirled around, disappointed, and jogged back to my team, ready to try again.

Reflect on Your Writing

Look back at the autobiography you wrote in Unit 3. Ask yourself these questions:

○ Did I use words that clearly describe each character's actions?

○ Did I use words that make the experience and events come alive to the reader?

○ Did I use complete sentences?

If you answer **No** to any of the questions, edit your autobiography.

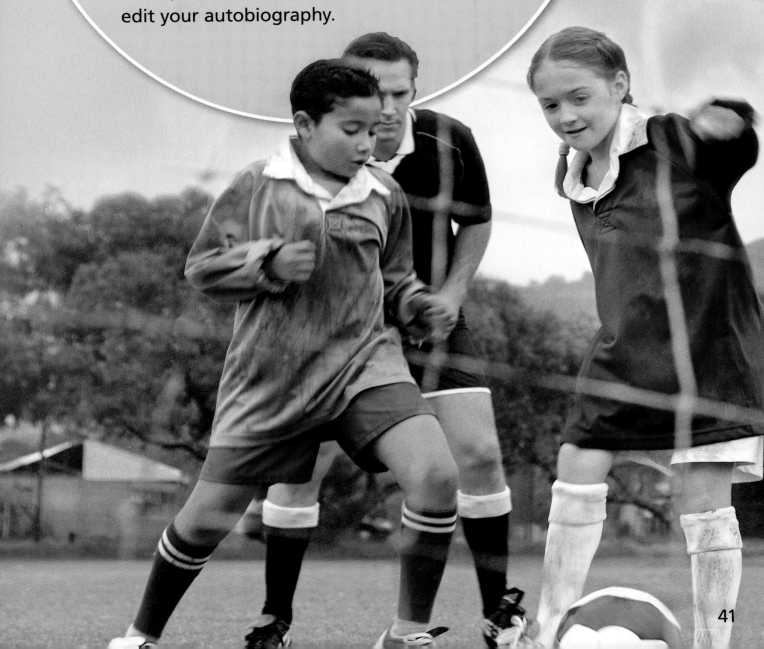

My Favorite Pet
My Smelly Pet

from **Judy Moody**

by Megan McDonald

illustrated by Peter H. Reynolds

My Favorite Pet

It was Labor Day, a no-school day. Judy looked up from her Me collage on the dining room table.

"We need a new pet," Judy announced to her family.

"A new pet? What's wrong with Mouse?" asked Mom. Mouse opened one eye.

"I have to pick MY FAVORITE PET. How can I pick my favorite when I only have one?"

"Pick Mouse," said Mom.

"Mouse is so old, and she's afraid of everything. Mouse is a lump that purrs."

"You're NOT thinking of a dog, I hope," said Dad. Mouse jumped off the chair and stretched.

"Mouse would definitely not like that," said Judy.

"How about a goldfish?" asked Stink. Mouse rubbed up against Judy's leg.

"Mouse would like that too much," Judy said. "I was thinking of a two-toed sloth."

"Right," said Stink.

"They're neat," said Judy. She showed Stink its picture in her rain forest magazine.

"See? They hang upside down all day. They even sleep upside down."

"You're upside down," said Stink.

"What do they eat?" asked Dad.

"It says here they eat leaf-cutter ants and fire-bellied toads," Judy read.

"That should be easy," said Stink.

"Tell you what, Judy," said Dad. "Let's take a ride over to the pet store. I'm not saying we'll get a sloth, but it's always fun to look around. Maybe it'll even help me think of a five-letter word for fish that starts with *M* for my crossword puzzle."

"Let's all go," said Mom.

When they arrived at Fur & Fangs, Judy saw snakes and parrots, hermit crabs and guppies. She even saw a five-letter fish word beginning with *M*—a black molly.

"Do you have any two-toed sloths?" she asked the pet store lady.

"Sorry. Fresh out," said the lady.

"How about a newt or a turtle?" asked Dad.

"Did you see the hamsters?" asked Mom.

"Never mind," said Judy. "There's nothing from the rain forest here."

"Maybe they have a stinkbug," Stink said.

"One's enough," said Judy, narrowing her eyes at Stink. They picked out a squeaky mouse toy for Mouse. When they went to pay for it, Judy noticed a green plant with teeth sitting on the counter. "What's that?" she asked the pet store lady.

"A Venus flytrap," the lady said. "It's not an animal, but it doesn't cost much, and it's easy to take care of. See these things that look like mouths with teeth? Each one closes like a trap door. It eats bugs around the house. Like flies and ants, that sort of thing. You can feed it a little raw hamburger too."

"Rare," said Judy Moody.

"Cool," said Stink.

"Good idea," said Mom.

"Sold," said Dad.

Judy set her new pet on her desk, where the angle of sunlight hit it just right. Mouse watched from the bottom bunk, with one eye open.

"I can't wait to take my new pet to school tomorrow for Share and Tell," Judy told Stink. "It's just like a rare plant from the rain forest."

"It is?" Stink asked.

"Sure," said Judy. "Just think. There could be a medicine hiding right here in these funny green teeth. When I'm a doctor, I'm going to study plants like this and discover cures for ucky diseases."

"What are you going to name it?" asked Stink.

"I don't know yet," said Judy.

"You could call it Bughead, since it likes bugs."

"Nah," said Judy.

Judy watered her new pet. She sprinkled Gro-Fast on the soil. When Stink left, she sang songs to it. "I know an old lady who swallowed a fly. . . ." She sang till the old lady swallowed a horse.

She still couldn't think of a good name.
Rumpelstiltskin? Too long. Thing? Maybe.

"Stink!" she called. "Go get me a fly."

"How am I going to catch a fly?" asked Stink.

"One fly. I'll give you a dime." Stink ran down to
the window behind the couch and brought back a fly.

"Gross! That fly is dead."

"It was going to be dead in a minute anyway."

Judy scooped up the dead fly with the tip of her
ruler and dropped it into one of the mouths. In a flash,
the trap closed around the fly. Just like the pet store
lady said.

"Rare!" said Judy.

"Snap! Trap!" Stink said, adding sound effects.

"Go get me an ant. A live one this time."

Here's one...

...a real beauty!

Here anty, anty!

No way!

Snap! Trap!

Urp!

50

Stink wanted to see the Venus flytrap eat again, so he got his sister an ant. "Snap! Trap!" said Judy and Stink when another trap closed.

"Double rare," Judy said.

"Stink, go catch me a spider or something."

"I'm tired of catching bugs," said Stink.

"Then go ask Mom or Dad if we have any raw hamburger."

Stink frowned.

"Please, pretty please with bubble-gum ice cream on top?" Judy begged. Stink didn't budge. "I'll let you feed it this time."

Stink ran to the kitchen and came back with a hunk of raw hamburger. He plopped a big glob of hamburger into an open trap.

"That's way too much!" Judy yelled, but it was too late. The mouth snap-trapped around it, hamburger oozing out of its teeth. In a blink, the whole arm drooped, collapsing in the dirt.

"You killed it! You're in trouble, Stink. MOM! DAD!" Judy called.

Judy showed her parents what happened. "Stink killed my Venus flytrap!"

"I didn't mean to," said Stink. "The trap closed really fast!"

"It's not dead. It's digesting," said Dad.

"The jaws will probably open by tomorrow morning," said Mom.

"Maybe it's just sleeping or something," said Stink.

"Or something," said Judy.

My Smelly Pet

Tomorrow morning came. The jaws were still closed. Judy tried teasing it with a brand new ant. "Here you go," she said in her best squeaky baby voice. "You like ants, don't you?" The jaws did not open one tiny centimeter. The plant did not move one trigger hair.

Judy gave up. She carefully lodged the plant in the bottom of her backpack. She'd take it to school, stinky, smelly glob of hamburger and all.

On the bus, Judy showed Rocky her new pet. "I couldn't wait to show everybody how it eats. Now it won't even move. And it smells."

"Open Sesame!" said Rocky, trying some magic words. Nothing happened.

"Maybe," said Rocky, "the bus will bounce it open."

"Maybe," said Judy. But even the bouncing of the bus did not make her new pet open up.

"If this thing dies, I'm stuck with Mouse for MY FAVORITE PET," Judy said.

Mr. Todd said first thing, "Okay, class, take out your Me collage folders. I'll pass around old magazines, and you can spend the next half-hour cutting out pictures for your collages. You still have over three weeks, but I'd like to see how everybody's doing."

Her Me collage folder! Judy had been so busy with her new pet, she had forgotten to bring her folder to school.

Judy Moody sneaked a peek at Frank Pearl's folder. He had cut out pictures of macaroni (favorite food?), ants (favorite pet?), and shoes. Shoes? Frank Pearl's best friend was a pair of shoes?

Judy looked down at the open backpack under her desk. The jaws were still closed. Now her whole backpack was smelly. Judy took the straw from her juice box and poked at the Venus flytrap. No luck. It would never open in time for Share and Tell!

"Well?" Frank asked.

"Well, what?"

"Are you going to come?"

"Where?"

"My birthday party. A week from Saturday. All
the boys from our class are coming. And Adrian and
Sandy from next door."

Judy Moody did not care if the president himself
was coming. She sniffed her backpack. It stunk like a
skunk!

"What's in your backpack?" Frank asked.

"None of your beeswax," Judy said.

"It smells like dead tuna fish!" Frank Pearl said.
Judy hoped her Venus flytrap would come back to
life and bite Frank Pearl before he ever had another
birthday.

Mr. Todd came over. "Judy, you haven't cut out any
pictures. Do you have your folder?"

"I did—I mean—it was—then—well—no," said Judy. "I got a new pet last night."

"Don't tell me," said Mr. Todd. "Your new pet ate your Me collage folder."

"Not exactly. But it did eat one dead fly and one live ant. And then a big glob of . . ."

"Next time try to remember to bring your folder to school, Judy. And please, everyone, keep homework away from animals!"

"My new pet's not an animal, Mr. Todd," Judy said. "And it doesn't eat homework. Just bugs and raw hamburger." She pulled the Venus flytrap from her backpack. Judy could not believe her eyes! Its arm was no longer droopy. The stuck trap was now wide open, and her plant was looking hungry.

"It's MY FAVORITE PET," said Judy. "Meet Jaws!"

Activity Central

Defined Online

In the chapter "My Favorite Pet," Judy asks Stink to get some bugs. At first Stink does not budge. If you don't know the meaning of the word *budge,* you can use an online dictionary to look up the meaning.

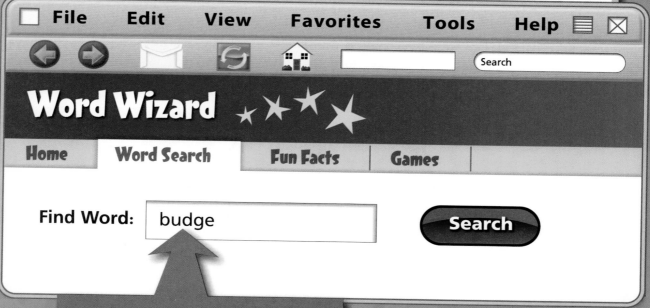

File   Edit   View   Favorites   Tools   Help

Search

Word Wizard ★★★★

| Home | Word Search | Fun Facts | Games |

Find Word: budge

Search

In the search box, type the word you want to look up. Click on the "Search" button or press the "Enter" key on the keyboard.

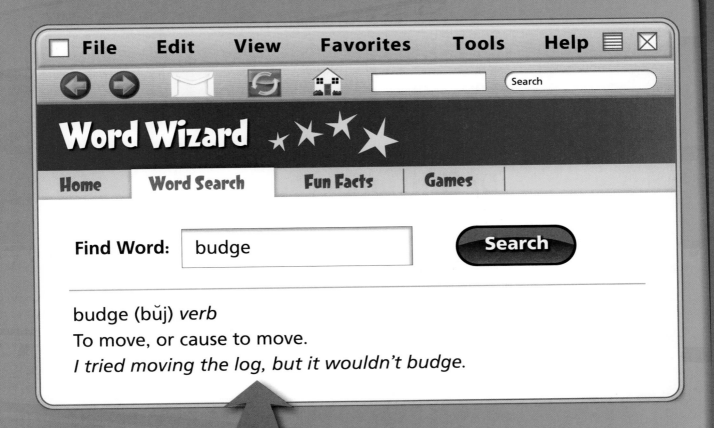

Word Wizard ★★★★

Home | Word Search | Fun Facts | Games

Find Word: budge

[Search]

budge (bŭj) *verb*
To move, or cause to move.
I tried moving the log, but it wouldn't budge.

Read the entry to find out what the word means. If there is more than one entry for a word, choose the meaning that matches the way the word is used in the selection.

Read the sentences. Use an online dictionary to find the meanings of the underlined words.

1. When they finished their meal at the restaurant, they paid for it at the <u>counter</u>.

2. The old mansion had a <u>trap door</u>.

3. The leaves of the plant were <u>droopy</u>.

4. The <u>trigger</u> hairs on the plant swayed toward the insect.

Your Turn

Let's Make Something Very Clear

Definitions

Good writers add definitions to explain the meaning of words that may not be familiar to their readers.

No Definition	Strong Definition
The Venus flytrap is a carnivorous plant.	The Venus flytrap is a carnivorous plant because it eats meat.

Why is the strong definition better? The word *carnivorous* is explained within the sentence as a word to describe something that eats meat.

Connecting Words

Good writers add connecting words, such as *also, another, and, more,* and *but* to link their ideas and make them clear to their readers.

Weak Link	Strong Link
You can feed a Venus flytrap flies and ants if you want to catch them. You can feed it hamburger.	You can feed a Venus flytrap flies and ants if you want to catch them. You can also feed it hamburger.

Why is the strong link better? It uses the word *also* to show that flies, ants, and hamburger are all foods you can feed a Venus flytrap.

Reflect On Your Writing

Choose a piece of your writing from Unit 4. Look it over. Ask yourself these questions:

▶ Where can I add definitions to explain the meaning of words that may not be familiar to my audience?

▶ Where can I use connecting words such as *and*, *but*, *then*, *also*, *another*, and *more* to link ideas?

Edit your writing to add definitions and connecting words to link ideas.

Writing Tip

When you revise your writing, it can be helpful to read your writing out loud. Hearing what you have written can help you notice places for improvement.

Ram's Angry Horns
A Myth from Nigeria

retold by Myka-Lynne Sokoloff
illustrated by Cindy Revell

◆◇◆◇◆◇◆◇◆◇◆◇◆◇◆◇◆◇◆◇◆◇◆

One fine spring day, when the world was new, Ewe gave birth to a lamb. Soon all of the villagers crowded around to admire her new lamb.

"What a handsome thing he is!" said Leopard. Gazelle also looked fondly at the young lamb.

"It's good to have new life in the village," said Elephant.

Hyena joked, "One day soon lamb will be running around the village, butting into everyone's business." The villagers all chuckled at the remark. No one knew how true Hyena's words would turn out to be.

Finally, the villagers left the new mother to rest peacefully with her lamb. "You will be called Ram," Ewe baaed softly. "You are the handsomest baby in all of Africa!"

Indeed, the lamb became more and more handsome as he grew. In fact, he was so handsome that he seemed to get his way with everyone, especially his mother. Ram thought only about himself. He never stopped to think about others.

In time, the other young animals in the village became very put out with Ram. They no longer wanted to play with him. When they saw Ram, the other animal children ran and hid.

Each day, from morning till night, Ram raced around the village causing trouble. Ram splashed in the water. He sprayed droplets of water on Hyena, who lounged in the sun on the shore. Ram hopped across the river stones. Then he ran boldly up and down Crocodile's back, from the tip of Crocodile's tail to the very end of his nose! He ran through the fields where others had just planted seeds. He rubbed his muddy coat against the clean laundry that hung on the line. He tracked mud through the hut where his mother had just swept the floor.

Ewe looked up from her chores and saw all the mischief Ram was making. She baaed gently to make her son stop, but he just pretended not to hear her. Ewe bleated and cried more strongly, until soon she was bellowing deeply and loudly. Ram continued to ignore his mother.

Ram had no friends, and his mother didn't know what to do with her selfish child. She truly wished he would learn some manners, but she had spoiled him beyond repair. Each time Ram misbehaved, the villagers shivered. They waited nervously for Ewe's loud bellows to begin.

Zebra covered her ears. Elephant winced in pain. Crocodile swam away. Flamingo flapped her wings wildly. Hyena would have laughed, but he didn't find Ram's tricks particularly funny.

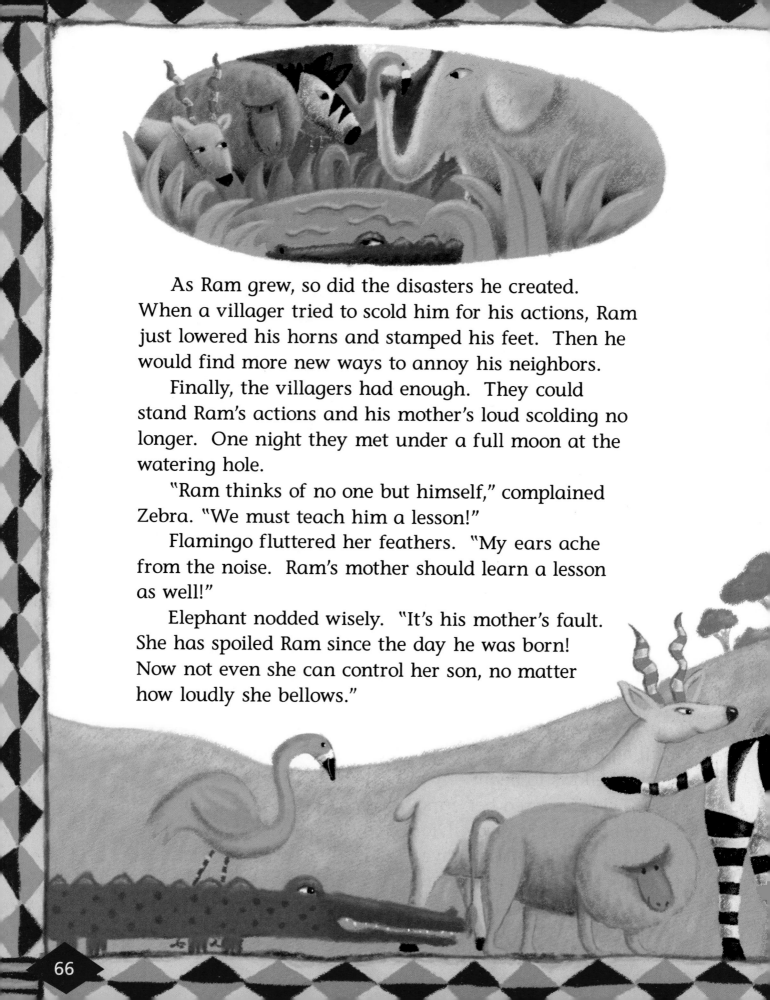

As Ram grew, so did the disasters he created. When a villager tried to scold him for his actions, Ram just lowered his horns and stamped his feet. Then he would find more new ways to annoy his neighbors.

Finally, the villagers had enough. They could stand Ram's actions and his mother's loud scolding no longer. One night they met under a full moon at the watering hole.

"Ram thinks of no one but himself," complained Zebra. "We must teach him a lesson!"

Flamingo fluttered her feathers. "My ears ache from the noise. Ram's mother should learn a lesson as well!"

Elephant nodded wisely. "It's his mother's fault. She has spoiled Ram since the day he was born! Now not even she can control her son, no matter how loudly she bellows."

"We have no choice," Baboon said. "We must send Ram and his mother away from the village. Otherwise, our homes and our children will constantly be in harm's way."

Soon the villagers agreed on a solution. They packed up Ram, his mother, and their belongings. They all formed a parade to escort Ram and Ewe to the edge of town. Ewe and Ram were to speak to no one in the village again.

"Ah, quiet," sighed Leopard as he lay down to doze in the soft, flat grass.

"Now we can get some rest," thought Elephant. It had been so long, she nearly forgot what a nice nap felt like.

"Peace at last," said Crocodile, grinning widely in the river.

The peace did not last long. Although Ram had no friends in the village, now that he was so far from others, he felt lonely. He was bored, too. Even outside of the village, Ewe could control her son no better than she could in the village.

One day Ram pawed at the dirt and kicked the grass. Ram got angrier and angrier as he stood there, feeling sorry for himself.

As Ram stared at the ground, he noticed something shiny. It was a piece of glass. That gave him an idea. He knew how he would get even with the animals in the village!

Ram held the glass so that it caught the sun's rays. It shone brightly on a clump of dried grass. Very quickly, the grass grew warm. Finally, it began to burn. Ram blew on the little flame with all his might.

Next, Ram shook his horned head as fast as he could to make the flames grow higher. He stood back and rubbed his hooves together with glee.

The flames raced toward the village. The fire burned up the grass where Leopard napped in the warm sun. Leopard escaped just in time! The flames licked the leafy trees where Cheetah liked to climb. Fortunately, Cheetah was off doing laundry at the river, so he wasn't hurt. Soon the fire dashed toward the huts that circled the center of the village.

"I smell smoke," Hyena giggled nervously.

Flamingo pointed one wing at the ball of fire that headed straight in their direction.

"Quick, everyone! We must do something!" screamed Baboon.

Elephant trumpeted to call the villagers together. Then she raced to the watering hole and filled her trunk to spray the flames. The other villagers carried baskets and gourds of water to put out the fire. By the time they finished, the watering hole was nearly dry. When night fell, the flames were out, but little remained of the village. Once again, the villagers met under the full moon.

"We put up with Ram's tricks when he was young," Leopard complained. "His mother just got noisier and noisier. We covered our ears to block the sound."

Baboon nodded. "Now Ram has ruined our food and burned our homes."

"We must send Ram and his mother even farther away," Elephant said. The villagers agreed, sadly, for they did not want to harm their neighbors.

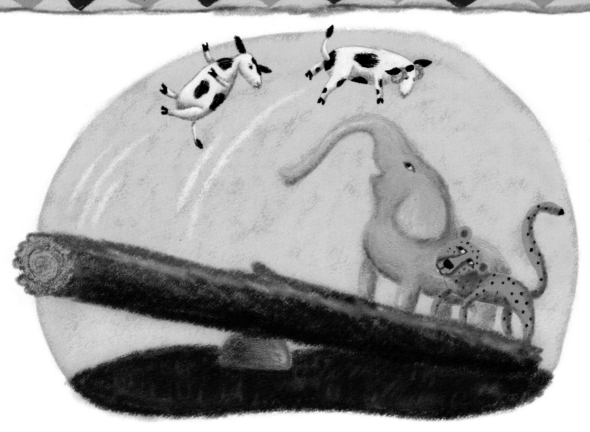

The villagers put their heads together and came up with a plan. They used a fallen tree trunk to build a giant seesaw. Ram and Ewe stood on one end. Elephant and Cheetah jumped on the other end. Ram and his mother flew high up into the clouds.

Now you may be wondering what happened to Ram and his mother. If you look and listen carefully next time a thunderstorm comes, you will find the answer in the sky.

Those lightning bolts? That's just Ram tossing balls of fire around the sky with his angry horns. That noise you call thunder? That's his mother, bellowing at her naughty son.

The sky will be their home forever. For that is where they belong, far away from the village, where they would surely make more trouble!

Read It! Record It!

Myths, such as *Ram's Angry Horns,* were first told by parents to their children or by storytellers a very long time ago.

Have you ever listened to a storyteller or to a story read aloud on a CD or podcast? These stories are told or read by someone who has practiced to make the story fun to listen to.

Choose a story or poem to read aloud.

1 Read the story or poem aloud a few times. Try out some different voices to make your characters come alive. Don't read too fast or too slowly.

2 Once you have practiced reading the story or poem, make a recording.

3 Listen to the recording, and make sure you like the way it sounds. If it's not as good as you would like, record it again.

4 Draw some pictures to make the details of the story or poem clearer to your listeners.

Be sure you
- Speak clearly.
- Vary your speed.
- Use lots of expression.

Then play your recording for your class and display your pictures. If your teacher has a class website, you may be able to post your recording and pictures for your friends and family to enjoy. Get ready to take a bow!

What Happens in the End?

A good story makes it easy for the reader to get to know the characters and what happens to them. A good story has a problem and gets the reader interested in how the characters solve the problem. Good writers make sure to tell how the problem is solved.

Ram's Angry Horns is fun to read because it has interesting characters that have to solve a problem. What is the problem? What happens at the end of *Ram's Angry Horns*? Does the ending tell how the problem is solved?

Reflect On Your Writing

Choose a story you wrote in Unit 5. As you read over your story, ask yourself these questions:

- What problem do the characters have?

- Did I organize the events in an order that makes sense?

- Is the problem solved in the end?

If you answer *No* to any of the questions, edit your story.

Credits